SPACE ACADEMY

ASTRONAUT

IN TRAINING

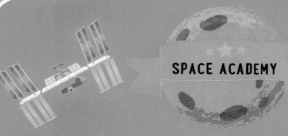

SPACE ACADEMY

STUDENT PASS

Name ....

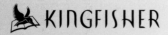KINGFISHER

First published 2018 by Kingfisher
an imprint of Macmillan Children's Books
20 New Wharf Road, London N1 9RR
Associated companies throughout the world
www.panmacmillan.com

Series editor: Hayley Down
Designer: Jeni Child
Author: Cath Ard
Illustrator: Sarah Lawrence
Consultant: Raman Prinja

ISBN 978-0-7534-4268-5

Copyright © Macmillan Publishers International Ltd 2018

9 8 7 6 5 4 3 2

2TR/0419/WKT/UG/128MA

A CIP catalogue record for this book is available from the British Library.

Printed in China

Picture credits
The Publisher would like to thank the following for permission to reproduce their material.
Top = t; Bottom = b; Centre = c; Left = l; Right = r
Pages 20 Shutterstock/solarseven; 24tr Shutterstock/Castleski; 38-39 Shutterstock/Triff; 42br Alamy/Granger Historical Picture Archive; 43tl Alamy/ITAR-TASS News Agency; all other photographs NASA.

ASTRONAUT
IN TRAINING

KINGFISHER

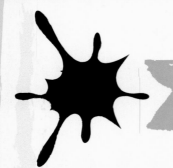

TRAINING PROGRAMME

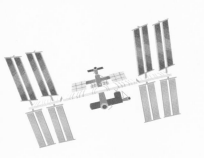

TRAINING TIME

So, you think you could be an astronaut? Are you calm in a crisis? Are you good at fixing things? Are you brave and adventurous? Then congratulations! You have been selected for astronaut training.

WORKOUT

As a trainee astronaut, you have to exercise for two hours a day. You need to be fit and strong to wear a heavy spacesuit on a six-hour spacewalk.

SPEAK RUSSIAN

You will blast off on board a Russian rocket, so you need to be able to read the writing on the rocket controls and understand people back at Russian **Mission Control**.

Practise these Russian words to get started:

Hi: Привет
(say "pree-vyet")

No: Нет
(say "nyet")

Yes: Да
(say "da")

Bye-bye: Пока
(say "pa-ka")

Russian has a different alphabet to English.

You need a strong stomach!

BUMPY RIDE

Take a rollercoaster ride in a special aeroplane! As it flies up and down through the air, you feel light and floaty for about 20 seconds – just like you will in space. Hold onto your lunch, though – astronauts call it the "Vomit Comet"!

FIRST-AID ACE

There are no hospitals in space, so you will have to look after yourself and your fellow astronauts if you get sick or injured.

Spot three differences between the two pictures.

PRACTICAL NO: 1

tick here

APPROVED

ADVANCED TRAINING

Well done! You passed the first part of your training with top marks. Now you are ready for the next part.

ROCKET ROOM

It's time to fly a rocket ... without leaving the ground! Astronauts use life-sized models, called **simulators**, to get to know their spacecraft's controls and to learn how to deal with emergencies that might happen in space.

..... NASA simulator

VIRTUAL REALITY

Plug in your virtual-reality headset and be magically transported to a space station. Take a tour around the different areas and practise the jobs you will have to do on your mission.

virtual-reality
headset

training for zero gravity

WATERY SPACEWALK

Put on your spacesuit and take a dip in a giant swimming pool! Moving about underwater is good training for the floaty feeling you will have in space.

Next time you go swimming, try to walk like an astronaut.

SPEEDY SPINNER

Take a spin in a machine called a **centrifuge**. It's like a super-fast fairground ride with only one seat. As you whizz around you are pushed back into your seat and your head and body feel horribly heavy. This is just how it feels when astronauts plunge back to the Earth at the end of a space mission.

Hold on tight!

Between the Earth's surface and space, there is a layer of air called

There is no air in space. Astronauts need to wear a spacesuit to help them breathe.

The International Space Station is about 350 kilometres above the Earth.

It only takes two minutes for a space rocket to reach the beginning of space.

350 km

the **atmosphere**. It changes the higher above the ground you travel.

Hot-air balloons drift along with the wind. The air is cooler up here.

The top of Mount Everest is the highest place on the Earth. It is hard to breathe at this height without wearing an oxygen mask.

The highest-flying aircraft travel a quarter of the way up into space.

WHERE IS SPACE?

Before you begin your mission, you need to know more about where you are going. Space lies a long way up above your head.

100 km

21 km

8848 m

THE NIGHT SKY

Take a break from training to gaze at the night sky. It is dotted with twinkling stars.

Some of the groups of stars make shapes in the sky. We call these shapes **constellations**.

JOIN-THE-STARS

Long ago, people named some constellations after heroes and creatures in their favourite stories. Can you find these constellations in the big picture?

O Cygnus is a swan

O Scorpus is a scorpion

O Leo is a lion

O Orion is a hunter

O Hercules is a hero

crescent Moon

half Moon

full Moon

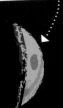

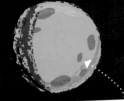

new Moon

quarter Moon

third-quarter Moon

🌙 MOON GAZING

The Moon travels around the Earth. The whole Moon is always in the sky, but often we can only see part of it, so it seems to change shape.

What shape is the Moon tonight?

PREPARE FOR LIFT-OFF!

Hooray! Launch day has finally arrived. There's a lot to do before you blast into space but the countdown clock is already ticking ...

GROUND CHECKS

While the ground crew and control room are busy checking the weather and preparing the rocket, you will be busy, too.

LAUNCH CHECKLIST

 ◯ Do an interview for the TV reporters.

 ◯ Put on the special suit you need to wear for launch and landing.

 ◯ Travel to the rocket in the Astrovan. (It's just a van for the astronauts!)

 ◯ Wave goodbye to your family, friends and fans.

 ◯ Take the lift to the top of the launch tower.

 ◯ Strap into your comfy seat in the tiny space module.

- 03 : 00 : 00

COUNTDOWN

The countdown happens backwards, so "T minus 2 minutes" means there are 2 minutes left until launch. The last ten seconds of the countdown are done on a loud speaker: ten, nine, eight, seven, six, five ...

LIFT-OFF!

Hear the rumbling roar as the engines start up. Feel the rocket shake as it blasts off and gathers speed ...

Fuel tank falls off and nose cone breaks away

booster rockets fall away

Next stop, space!

Boosters blast off

FALL OFF!

You will hear loud BANGS as parts of the rocket fall away. Don't panic! The astronauts are safe in the tiny module at the top. The fuel tanks, nose cone and other parts fall away when they have done their job.

THE SUN

Swot up on some facts as you journey into space. Every astronaut needs to know about the Sun. It's an ordinary star, but it's special to us because its rays light up our planet and keep us warm.

SIZE
Huge. You could fit over 1 million planet Earths inside the Sun. It looks small to us because it is far away.

KEY

Can you spot these things in the big picture?

- ○ **Surface:** the surface of the Sun is not solid. It is burning gas.
- ○ **Solar flares:** big curling flames bigger than the Earth that fly off into space.
- ○ **Sunspots:** cooler areas on the Sun's surface that look dark.
- ○ **Solar probe:** a spacecraft without any astronauts that collects information about the Sun.

STAY SAFE IN SPACE

Just like on the Earth, you will need to protect your eyes from the Sun's bright rays when you are in space.

- Pull down the tinted visor on your spacesuit when you go on spacewalks.

- Wear your sunglasses inside the spacecraft when you look out of the windows.

TEMPERATURE

The Sun's surface temperature is 5500 degrees Celsius. A really hot oven is only 250 degrees Celsius.

DISTANCE

The Sun is 150 million kilometres from the Earth. It would take a super-fast spacecraft over 150 days to reach it.

THEORY NO: 3
tick here
APPROVED

THE SOLAR SYSTEM

The Solar System is made up of the Sun and the eight planets that travel around it. The Earth is one of them!

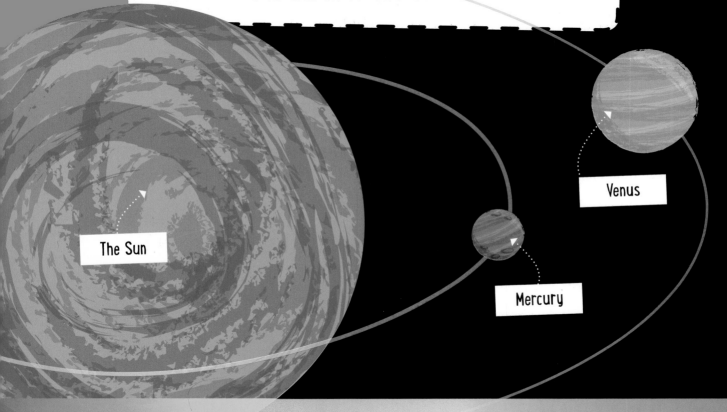

The Sun

Venus

Mercury

MERCURY
Boiling hot

The side that faces the Sun is roasting hot. The other side is f-f-f-freezing.

VENUS
Too hot

This hot planet is covered with thick clouds and extinct volcanoes.

EARTH
Perfect temperature

Our planet is the only one where animals and plants can live.

MARS
Too cold

This red planet is often covered in swirling dust storms.

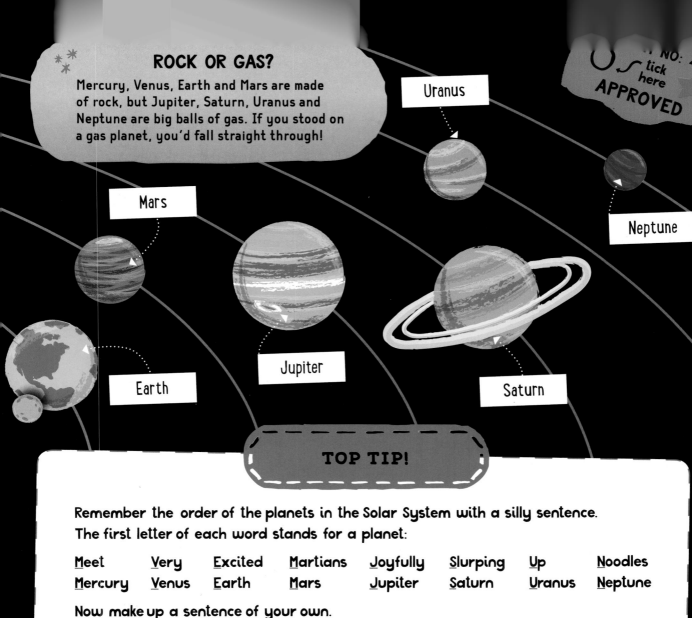

ROCK OR GAS?

Mercury, Venus, Earth and Mars are made of rock, but Jupiter, Saturn, Uranus and Neptune are big balls of gas. If you stood on a gas planet, you'd fall straight through!

Uranus

Neptune

Mars

Earth

Jupiter

Saturn

TOP TIP!

Remember the order of the planets in the Solar System with a silly sentence.
The first letter of each word stands for a planet:

Meet	Very	Excited	Martians	Joyfully	Slurping	Up	Noodles
Mercury	Venus	Earth	Mars	Jupiter	Saturn	Uranus	Neptune

Now make up a sentence of your own.

M.............. V.............. E.............. M.............. J.............. S.............. U.............. N..............

JUPITER
Colder

This is the largest planet in the Solar System. It has 67 moons.

SATURN
Colder still

This planet is surrounded by rings of rock and ice.

URANUS
Brrr

Uranus is made of icy material that flows around its rocky centre.

NEPTUNE
Freezing cold

This icy blue planet has the strongest winds in the Solar System.

DWARF PLANETS

A dwarf planet, such as Ceres, is a ball of rock covered in ice. Pluto is the Solar System's largest dwarf planet, but it's smaller than our Moon.

Ceres

METEORITES

Meteoroids are tiny bits of space rock. When one comes close to the Earth and starts to burn, we call it a meteor. If it crashes to the ground without burning up, it's a meteorite!

THEORY 5

SMALL STUFF

As well as planets, there are other, smaller things whizzing around in space. Some are giant pieces of rock and ice, and some are tiny specks of dust.

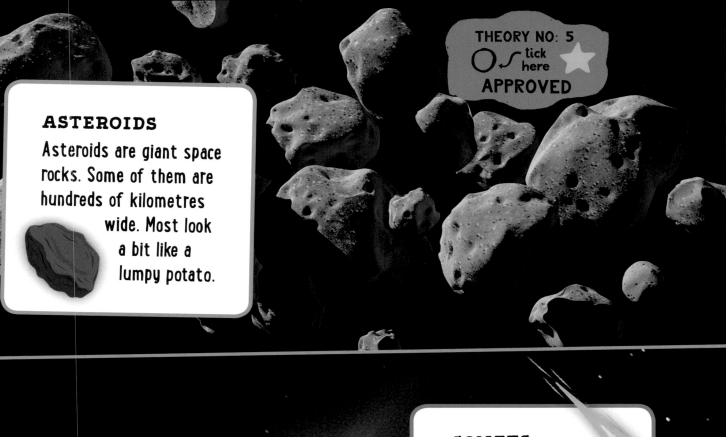

THEORY NO: 5
tick here
APPROVED

ASTEROIDS

Asteroids are giant space rocks. Some of them are hundreds of kilometres wide. Most look a bit like a lumpy potato.

COMETS

A comet is a huge chunk of dirty ice. As it flies past the Sun, it heats up and a tail of glowing gas trails out behind it.

Comet Lovejoy

HOW TO SPOT A SHOOTING STAR

When people see a shooting star, it is really a meteor! There are lots of regular meteor showers to look out for – the Perseids happen between 17th July and 24th August every year.

THE MOON

Put on your spacesuit and prepare for landing – you have arrived at the Moon! This is the Earth's closest neighbour and the first destination in your space training.

Find your way around the Moon to the finish.

Start

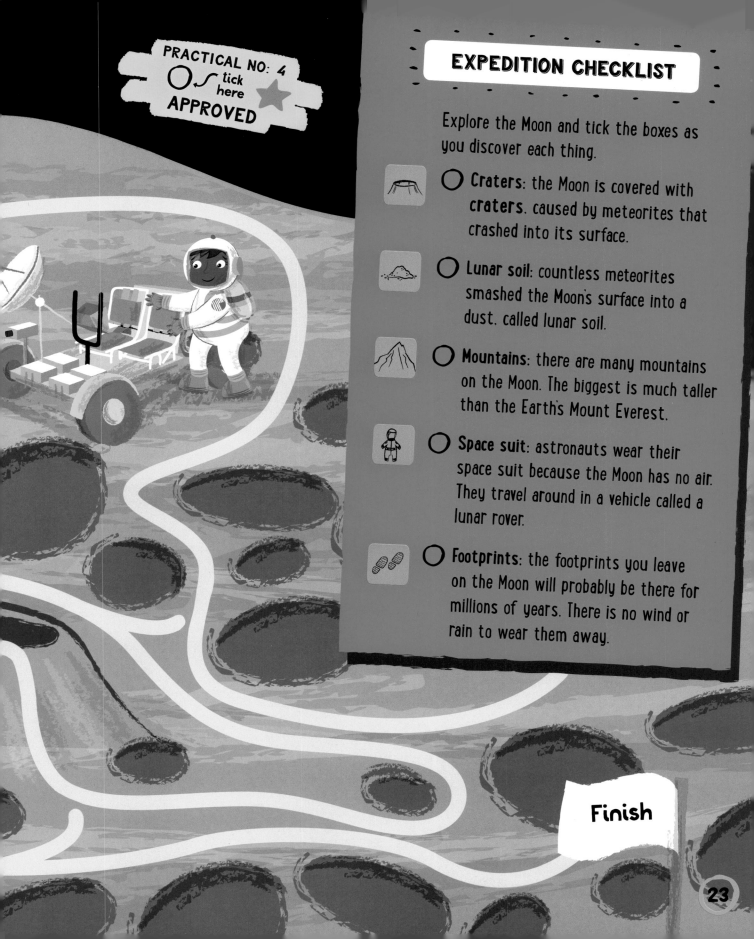

EXPEDITION CHECKLIST

Explore the Moon and tick the boxes as you discover each thing.

○ **Craters:** the Moon is covered with **craters,** caused by meteorites that crashed into its surface.

○ **Lunar soil:** countless meteorites smashed the Moon's surface into a dust, called lunar soil.

○ **Mountains:** there are many mountains on the Moon. The biggest is much taller than the Earth's Mount Everest.

○ **Space suit:** astronauts wear their space suit because the Moon has no air. They travel around in a vehicle called a lunar rover.

○ **Footprints:** the footprints you leave on the Moon will probably be there for millions of years. There is no wind or rain to wear them away.

Finish

1942

The German rocket V2 was the first object made by humans to reach space – 100 kilometres above the Earth's surface.

1961

Russian astronaut, Yuri Gagarin, became the first human in space. He flew for 108 minutes in his Vostok 1 spacecraft.

1957

Sputnik was the first **satellite** sent into space. This small metal ball travelled around the Earth making a beeping noise that could be heard by radio operators all over the world.

1957

Laika the Russian space dog became the first animal to orbit the Earth in her spacecraft Sputnik 2.

THEORY 6

SPACE MISSIONS

Thousands of rockets have blasted off on space missions over the years. Find out how it all began ...

1969

The first astronauts walked on the Moon. They returned safely in their spacecraft, Apollo 11. The Moon is the only object in space that humans have visited.

2000

The first crew of astronauts moved into the International Space Station.

1981

The space shuttle was the first spacecraft to be used more than once. It could land safely on a runway, just like an aeroplane. Five space shuttles made a total of 135 space flights.

2019

China's Chang'e 4 is the first mission to successfully land on the far side of the Moon – the side that always faces away from Earth.

YOUR MISSION

Add your space mission to this list:

Date:

Rocket name:

THEORY NO: 6

tick here

APPROVED

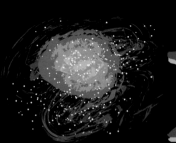

GALAXIES

ELLIPTICAL GALAXIES

From the Earth, these bright balls look like one big star in the night sky because the stars are clustered together.

IRREGULAR GALAXIES

These can look like clouds, splats, smudges or strange squiggles.

Some of the lights you see in the night sky are not stars, but galaxies. Galaxies are made of billions of stars grouped together. They come in different shapes and sizes.

SPIRAL GALAXIES

Spiral galaxies have arms that curl out from a big group of stars in the middle.

MILKY WAY

The Earth, the Sun and all the planets in our Solar System are inside a spiral galaxy called the Milky Way.

Look up on a clear night and see if you can spot the Milky Way.

You are here!

THEORY NO: 7

tick here

1. CATCH IT IF YOU CAN!

The ISS **orbits** the Earth. Blast your spacecraft into orbit, just ahead of the ISS.

2. GET CLOSER ...

Now you're on the same orbit path as the ISS, slow down to let the ISS catch up.

PRACTICAL 5

DESTINATION ISS

Hooray! There's the space station where you're going to live. All you have to do is park up and step inside. Easy, right?

ON OFF

3. GET CONNECTED

Line up with the ISS **docking port** and slow down until you're connected.

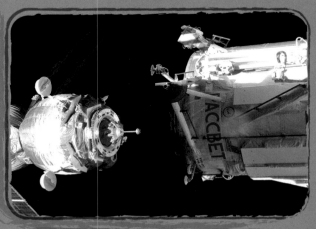

EJECT

4. YOU MADE IT!

Phew! Now open the hatch and float through to meet the space station crew.

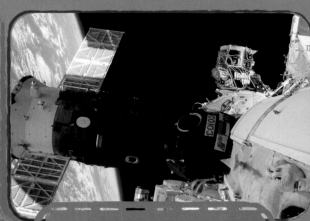

ACTIVITY

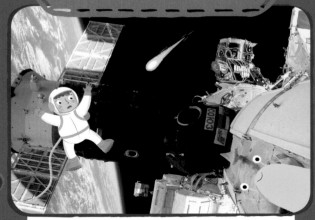

Spot three differences between the two pictures.

FAST

ON THE EARTH ... your feet stay firmly on the floor – unless you trip up ... then you fall down.

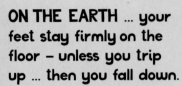

IN SPACE ... inside a spacecraft you float. You need to hook your feet under rails or loops to keep still.

HAIR UP

ON THE EARTH ... long hair hangs down, pulled by gravity. You need hairbands or gel to hold it up.

IN SPACE ... long hair floats up because there is very little gravity.

THEORY 8

GRAVITY

avity is an invisible force that pulls you to the ground on Earth. There isn't much gravity in space, so you will float!

DRINK UP

ON THE EARTH ... pour a glass of water and gravity pulls it down into the glass.

IN SPACE ... liquid floats around in blobs, so drinks have to be slurped through a straw or gobbled.

TIDY UP

ON THE EARTH ... you can drop your clothes on the bedroom floor and they stay there until you pick them up.

IN SPACE ... everything needs to be held down with clips, sticky tape, magnets and Velcro or the space station becomes full of floating mess.

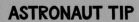

ASTRONAUT TIP

Floating about in space can make you feel sick. Your tummy doesn't know which way is up - or down! Keep some sick bags handy.

THEORY NO: 8

tick here

APPROVED

LIVING IN SPACE

Now you're on board the ISS. Let's take a tour.

DINNER'S UP

The ISS is jam-packed with food pouches. Just add water or heat them up and dinner's served!

Tasty!

WASH UP

No bubble baths here! If your feet start to smell, you'll need to use a wet towel and soap to wash them!

ZZZZZZ

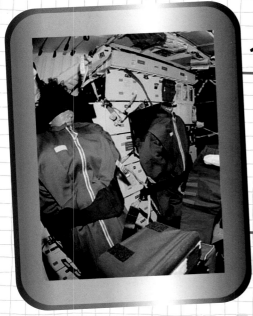

GO BUMP IN THE NIGHT ...

Here's an ISS bedroom - see the sleeping bag strapped to the wall? It stops you from floating away in the night!

Yuk!

docking port

WORK UP A SWEAT

You need to keep fit to be an astronaut. Make sure you do regular workouts.

WASTE IN SPACE!

The toilet on the ISS has a hosepipe to suck up your number ones and a seat with a sucking hole for your number twos.

ACTIVITY

Can you find the following rooms:

◯ Kitchen   ◯ Bedroom

◯ Gym   ◯ Toilet

EXPERIMENTS

Astronauts do experiments on plants, animals and their own body to see what happens to them in space.

You might grow plants, such as lettuce, peas and radishes.

PRACTICAL 7

WORKING IN SPACE

It's time to get to busy! The space station is like a giant laboratory, where astronauts from different countries work.

CHORES

You will spend time fixing broken parts, testing computers and doing safety checks to make sure everything is working perfectly. You will also spend time vacuuming and cleaning to keep the space station spic and span.

Collect samples of your spit, blood and skin - yuck!

Study worms, ants, bees and mice to see how they behave in space.

ACTIVITY

Can you find these things on the ISS?

lettuce

spanner

head phones

PHOTOS

Take plenty of pics of life on board and amazing views of the Earth out of the windows. Upload them to the Internet for people back home to see.

✳✳ CUPOLA

The cupola is a big window on the ISS that lets astronauts look down on the Earth.

CALL HOME

You may be hundreds of kilometres above the Earth, but you still need to keep in touch with everyone back home.

GIVE US A WAVE

Spacecraft communicate with the Earth using radio waves – the invisible signals that carry information to our TVs, radios and mobile phones. Big satellite dishes all over the world collect the radio waves sent from space.

Hi, Mum!

FAMILY CHAT

When you're on the space station, you can talk to your family on a special phone. You can even make a video call.

IS ANYONE OUT THERE?

The space station sends out a radio wave, which needs to travel around the Earth to Mission Control. A satellite dish on the Earth picks up the radio wave. It bounces the wave up to a satellite in space, which bounces it back to another dish on the Earth. Up and down the radio wave goes, until it reaches Mission Control.

ACTIVITY

When two waves meet, we get interference. Turn on your radio and put a mobile phone near it – does the sound go crackly? That's the radio waves interrupting each other!

MISSION CONTROL

Back on the Earth, there is a room full of people using computers to keep track of your mission. It is called Mission Control. It takes charge of lots of things on the ISS – even turning on the lights every morning!

The ISS has a robot arm, which astronauts control from the inside.

SPACE JUNK

Try not to drop anything when you are on a spacewalk. Nuts, bolts and screws that fly off into space can never be collected.

The longest ever spacewalk lasted over 9 hours.

PRACTICAL 8

SPACEWALK!

Sometimes astronauts leave the ISS to go on spacewalks. They make repairs or carry out experiments in space!

Your spacesuit gives you air to breathe and keeps you warm. It is also bulky and hard to move in.

Try brushing your teeth with your fluffiest gloves on!

The tether is a cable that attaches you to the ISS, so you don't float away!

TOOLKIT

These astronauts are replacing missing parts on the ISS. Can you see these shapes in the picture?

PRACTICAL NO: 8

tick here

APPROVED

PRACTICAL 9

DOWN TO EARTH

Your mission is over and it's time to head home. Returning to the Earth is called **re-entry** – and it's a bumpy ride!

RE-ENTRY CHECKLIST

○ Pack your belongings and samples from your science experiments into the spacecraft.

○ Put on the special spacesuit you wore for the launch.

○ Wave goodbye to your friends on the space station.

○ Climb into the **descent module** and close the hatch.

○ Snuggle down in your seat and strap in tight.

○ Wait for Mission Control to give the signal.

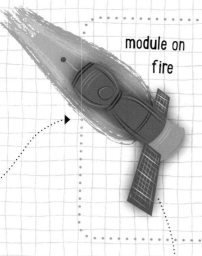

module on fire

BURN

When you leave space, your module is going so fast it catches fire, but you are protected inside.

You're in the middle module.

BUST

BANG! BANG! That's the spacecraft breaking into pieces. Don't panic – you don't need the bits that fall off. Only the descent module makes it home.

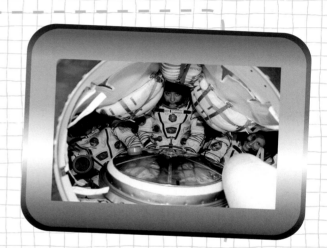

BREAK AGAIN

A parachute opens to slow down your fall.

Don't worry! It's safe.

CRASH!

You reach the ground, or the ocean. The hatch opens and ground crew help you out.

PRACTICAL NO: 9
tick here
APPROVED

ALEXEY LEONOV

This Russian cosmonaut did the first ever spacewalk. He floated in space for 12 minutes.

LAIKA

A Russian dog became the first animal to orbit the Earth in a spacecraft.

STEPHEN HAWKING

Stephen Hawking was a space expert. He made important discoveries about how the universe began.

LIU YANG

Liu Yang became the first female Chinese astronaut to go into space. She launched off in June 2012 with two other crew members.

HALL OF FAME

VALENTINA TERESHKOVA

Valentina is famous for being the first woman in space. She orbited the earth 48 times and took lots of photos.

YURI GAGARIN

This Russian cosmonaut became the first man in space. He travelled once around the Earth.

NEIL ARMSTRONG

This American astronaut is one of the most famous people that has ever lived. He was the first person to walk on the Moon!

GUION S. BLUFORD JR.

Guion was the first African American in space. He was also part of the first eight-person spaceflight in a single spacecraft!

These space travellers all made history with their cosmic adventures. Will you be next on the wall?

EXAMINATION

Now it's time to see how much you have learned.

1 How far above the Earth is the International Space Station?
a) 3 km
b) 35 km
c) 350 km

2 Which of these is the name of a constellation?
a) Cygnus
b) Cygnal
c) Swanus

3 How many planets are in the Solar System?
a) 2
b) 8
c) 28

4 What do the planets in the Solar System travel around?
a) The Sun
b) A galaxy
c) The Moon

5 What are asteroids and meteors?
a) planets
b) space rocks
c) rockets

6 What are the big holes in the Moon called?
a) grottos
b) graters
c) craters

7 Which of these sentences is TRUE?
a) It is very windy on the Moon.
b) It is never windy on the Moon.
c) It is sometimes windy on the Moon.

8 What is the name of the galaxy that the Earth sits inside?
a) The Galactic Way
b) The Minty Way
c) The Milky Way

9 Which of these sentences is FALSE?
a) The International Space Station travels around the Earth.
b) The International Space Station stays in the same place in space.

10 When you see a shooting star, what are you really looking at?
a) a comet
b) a dwarf planet
c) a meteor

11 What is the name of the invisible force that sticks you to the ground on the Earth?
a) groundity
b) heavily
c) gravity

12 Which of these things happens to you in space?
a) you float
b) you sink
c) you shrink

13 What is the name of the place back on the Earth where space missions are controlled?
a) Cosmic Control
b) Spacecraft Control
c) Mission Control

14 What is it called when an astronaut leaves the spacecraft in space?
a) a spacewalk
b) a spacehike
c) a spaceflight

SPACE SCORES

Check your answers at the back of the book and add up your score.

1 to 5 You need to swat up on your space facts before you go on another mission.

6 to 10 With a bit more study and training you could make a great astronaut.

11 to 14 Top of the class! You will make a first-class astronaut.

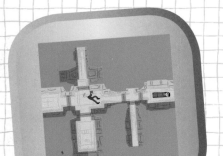

SPACE SPEAK

atmosphere
The layer of gases that surrounds a planet. The atmosphere on the Earth is called air.

centrifuge
A machine that spins around very quickly.

cosmonaut
The Russian name for someone who travels into space.

crater
A hole on the surface of a moon or planet, usually caused by space rocks crashing into it.

descent module
The part of a spacecraft that is used to return to the Earth.

docking port
A place where spacecraft can join onto a space station.

Milky Way
The name of the galaxy that our Solar System is in.

Mission Control
A room on the Earth where people communicate with spacecraft and space stations.

module
A part of a spacecraft.

orbit
To travel around a planet or star on a curved route, called an orbit path. The Earth orbits the Sun.

re-entry
When a spacecraft travels back into the Earth's atmosphere.

satellite
An object made mby humans that travels around a planet or through space.

simulator
A machine that recreates a scene or situation. so people can practise doing a job.

SPACE ACADEMY

WELL DONE!

You have completed your first successful space mission.

Name..

FULLY QUALIFIED

ASTRONAUT

ANSWERS

Page 7
The three differences are:

Page 13
The constellations are circled in the picture below.

Cygnus is circled in green.
Scorpus is circled in blue.
Leo is circled in red.
Orion is circled in pink.
Hercules is circled in purple.

Page 16
The things to find are circled below.

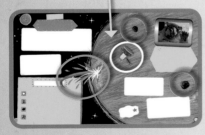

The surface is all of the outside of the Sun - see the yellow arrow.
The solar flare is circled in green.
The sunspots are circled in blue.
The solar probe is circled in white.

Page 22

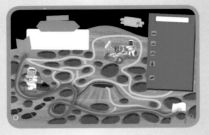

Page 29
The three differences are:

Page 32
The things to find are circled below.

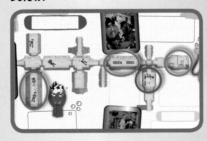

The kitchen is circled in green.
The gym is circled in blue.
The bedroom is circled in red.
The toilet is circled in pink.

Page 34
The things to find are circled below.

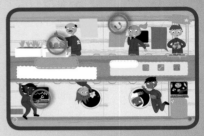

Page 38
The missing parts are circled below.

Page 44
1 = c; 2 = a; 3 = b; 4 = a;
5 = b; 6 = c; 7 = b; 8 = c;
9 = b; 10 = c; 11 = c; 12 = a;
13 = c; 14 = a.